Peer Pressure

"How Can I Say No?"

by Kate Havelin

Consultant:
Jennifer Griffin-Wiesner
Search Institute

Perspectives on Relationships

LifeMatters
an imprint of Capstone Press
Mankato, Minnesota

LifeMatters books are published by Capstone Press
818 North Willow Street • Mankato, Minnesota 56001
http://www.capstone-press.com

Printed in the United States of America

Library of Congress Cataloging-in-Publication Data
Havelin, Kate, 1961–
    Peer pressure: how can I say no? / by Kate Havelin.
        p. cm. — (Perspectives on relationships)
    Includes bibliographical references and index.
    Summary: Discusses different kinds of pressures exerted on young people by their peers, how these pressures can affect people, and ways to handle peer pressure.
    ISBN 0-7368-0291-6 (book). — ISBN 0-7368-0295-9 (series)
    1. Peer pressure—Juvenile literature. 2. Peer pressure—in Adolescence—Juvenile literature. [1. Peer pressure.] I. Title.
    II. Series.
    HQ784.P43H38 2000
    303.3´27—DC21   99-31166
                                  CIP

YA
305.235

Staff Credits
Katie Bagley, Kristin Thoennes, editors; Adam Lazar, designer; Heidi Schoof, photo researcher

Photo Credits
Cover: The Stock Market/©Gabe Palmer
FPG International/©Telegraph Colour Library, 9; ©Ron Chapple, 39
©Index Stock Photography, 49
International Stock/©Scott Barrow, 11, 22, 56, 57; ©Bill Stanton, 24; ©Dusty Willison, 51; ©Mitch Diamond, 59
Photo Network/©Esbin-Anderson, 15, 46; ©Myrleen Cate, 16, 34; ©Jeff Greenberg, 25, 31
Photri-Microstock/©Tom & Dee Ann McCarthy, 27
©RubberBall Productions, 58
Unicorn Stock Photos/©Eric R. Berndt, 33; ©Martin R. Jones, 43; ©Robert Ginn, 50
Visuals Unlimited/©Jeff Greenberg, 53

A 0 9 8 7 6 5 4 3 2 1

This book provided by a
grant from the
Family Resource Council
Merced County
Office of Education

Table of Contents

1	What Is Peer Pressure?	4
2	Why Does Peer Pressure Happen?	12
3	Is Peer Pressure All Bad?	20
4	The Pressure to Look Right	28
5	The Pressure to Act Cool	36
6	Dealing With Peer Pressure	44
7	Important Stuff to Remember	54
	Glossary	60
	For More Information	61
	Useful Addresses and Internet Sites	62
	Index	63

Chapter Overview

Peer pressure is the influence or power that people your own age have over you.

Peer pressure can be obvious or subtle. Sometimes peer pressure even comes from inside you.

There are many kinds of peer pressure, such as name-calling, put-downs, ostracization, and guilt games.

Almost everyone feels peer pressure.

Chapter 1

What Is Peer Pressure?

Do you ever feel like you are different from everyone else? Has anyone ever pushed you to do something you didn't want to do? Have you ever been afraid to do or say something because your friends might laugh at you? Has anyone ever made fun of you because of your clothes, your looks, or something you did?

Many teens feel the need to conform—to fit in. They feel like they have to be like everyone else. They may feel pressure to act in certain ways just to go along with others. This feeling is peer pressure.

Peers are the people who are your own age. They may be other students, coworkers, teammates, or neighbors. Some are friends, and some are just teens you know. Pressure is the influence or power that other people exert over you.

Peer pressure can be very powerful. It can affect your attitudes and behaviors. You may think that you make your own choices. However, peer pressure is usually a big reason why people do things.

Some peer pressure can be harmful. Chapters 4 and 5 discuss some kinds of negative peer pressure. However, some peer pressure can be good. Chapter 3 talks about positive peer pressure.

Different Kinds of Pressure

Some peer pressure is obvious. It is direct and easy to recognize. Everyone is smoking. They push a cigarette in your hand and urge you to smoke. Or someone starts making fun of your new sweater, and others join in. You are so embarrassed that you never wear the sweater again.

> "If you wear something that the other kids will laugh at, or if you sit in something or get caught, you know, having your period, then the whole class will see and make fun of you. It's nerve-wracking. Someone is always saying something. Someone is always watching. You have to be so careful."
> —an anonymous middle-school girl

Quote

Peer pressure may be friendly or hostile. A friend may invite you to cheat on a test with him or her. If you refuse, however, he or she may get angry. Your friend may accuse you of being selfish or of acting like you're better than everyone else.

Some peer pressure is more casual. For example, a friend may have shoplifted something at the mall. Your other friends are talking about how easy and cool it is. You think it's wrong to shoplift, but you don't want to say anything. You don't want to sound preachy. You don't want to be the only one who disagrees.

Pressure may be very subtle. For example, you may see many classmates wearing a certain style of jeans. This may influence you when you go shopping. You may decide that you want a pair of those jeans. People who never said anything to you about jeans influenced your choice of jeans.

Some peer pressure even comes from inside you. You may feel different from everyone else, even if no one says anything. For example, you may think that everyone is dating except you. This may make you feel left out. You may wish that you had a boyfriend or a girlfriend just so you could fit in.

Sometimes my friends can be so nasty. One
time our school had spirit week. We all

Anja, Age 15

thought it was kind of stupid, except for Carmel. She got all
dressed up in this crazy outfit in the school colors. Everyone
started making fun of her and she started to get really
embarrassed. I thought she was going to start crying, so I told
her I thought it was great that she was so enthusiastic. I was
just trying to be nice, but I don't think my friends liked it that I
said that. They gave me nasty looks and then just started
ignoring both of us. Later, I overheard two of them saying all
this mean stuff about us to these other guys.

Ways That Teens Are Pressured

Peer pressure happens in many ways. Some common forms of
direct peer pressure are name-calling, put-downs, ostracization,
and guilt games.

Name-Calling

"Geek!" "Dumb jock!" "Slut!" "Loser!"

People often use mean names to make fun of, or harass, people.
The names may not be true, but they hurt anyway. The sting of
labels lasts a long time.

Most teens face harassment at some point. Often, the harassment
has nothing to do with you personally. Most harassment is random
and unplanned. The people who harass others may barely know
their victims.

Put-Downs

"I can't believe you don't know that. You must be so stupid." "Did you get that shirt at a garage sale?" "You've never been to a concert? Where have you been?"

Sometimes it feels like everyone knows something except you. It may seem like everyone does something that you don't. Or you say the wrong thing or wear the wrong clothes. No one wants to feel dumb or different. Put-downs make people feel embarrassed or stupid.

Ostracization

"Hey, what are you doing here? This is our table. Go eat somewhere else."

Some groups ostracize, or exclude, outsiders. They make fun of teens who are not part of their group. Some groups won't even talk to outsiders. Sometimes, a group may even begin to exclude one of its own members.

Guilt Games

"C'mon, you can't stay home and study. We need a fifth person to play basketball. We'll lose if you don't play. What's more important—a little math test or your friends?"

Even good friends can make a person feel bad sometimes. Your friends may make you feel guilty. You may feel like you are disloyal to them if you don't do what they want.

"Sometimes you feel like you're different from everyone else. But the thing is, everyone feels different. If you look at the really popular people at your school, they feel pressure too. They probably don't have it together any more than you do. They may just look like they do. Sometimes the pressure doesn't seem so strong if you realize that everyone feels the same way."
—Kareem, age 17

There are other ways that teens are pressured. For example, your peers may spread rumors about you or talk about you behind your back if you do something they don't like. You even may be physically harassed.

Luis, Age 14

I used to like hanging out with my friends. Now it's really stressful. They're always daring each other to do stuff. Sometimes it's illegal or dangerous, but mostly it's just mean or stupid. I don't really want to go along with them, but I don't want them to think I'm a total loser either. So I usually end up going along with whatever they do. Sometimes I'll even think of something we could do, so it's my idea.

I hear a lot about peer pressure. But I'm not sure if this is pressure or not. It's not like they're forcing me to go along.

Recognizing Peer Pressure

Sometimes it's easy to tell you're being pressured. It may be obvious when others are pushing you to do something that you don't want to do. Sometimes it's more subtle. You may be afraid that others will make fun of you if you don't go along. You may feel uncomfortable with what you are being urged to do.

Peer Pressure

You may go along with others but later feel bad about what you did. You may not think much at all about what you want to do. Instead, you just do what others are doing without considering if it's right or wrong.

Peer pressure may make you feel out of place. You may feel very self-conscious. It may feel like everyone is looking at you.

Peer Pressure Happens to Everyone

Everyone feels peer pressure. Even adults feel some pressure. Everyone wants to fit in and have friends. Most people don't want to be too different. Most teens worry about what others think of them. You even may put pressure on someone else.

Points to Consider

What kinds of peer pressure have you experienced? What were you pressured to do?

What kinds of peer pressure do you think are most common?

How do you feel when you think that everyone is looking at you?

Have you ever put pressure on someone else? Why did you do that? How do you think that person felt?

Chapter Overview

Peer pressure may be especially strong during adolescence.

Puberty causes major physical and emotional changes. Teens also face many social changes.

A teen's relationships with his or her parents often changes. Friends usually become more important.

Sometimes teens pressure others so they can feel better about themselves.

It is natural to want to be part of a group, to belong.

Chapter 2

Why Does Peer Pressure Happen?

Everyone faces peer pressure. However, pressure may be especially strong during adolescence. Puberty causes major changes in a teen's body. Teens may not realize that everyone else is going through similar changes. This may make them feel strange or different. Puberty also brings important changes in a teen's thinking and personality. All of these changes are normal and necessary. However, the changes may be frightening, confusing, or difficult. They may make teens more self-conscious and unsure.

"Middle school was pretty tough. I started developing a chest before anyone else I knew, and it was really embarrassing. Guys would snap my bra and say all these sexual things to me. I hated how they would look at me. It seemed like I was crying all the time because of the stuff people said. It was funny, though, because a few years later the guys were making fun of the girls who were still flat-chested."
—Mariyah, age 17

Physical Changes

Puberty usually starts between the ages of 9 and 15, but it may start earlier or later. Girls usually start puberty before boys do. During puberty, teens grow rapidly. Not all parts of their body grow at the same time. They may become clumsy or awkward, which can be frustrating or embarrassing. Clothes may not fit right. For example, sleeves may be too short.

Other physical changes also may upset a teen. Both males and females grow body hair and sweat more. Some teens get acne, or pimples. A male's voice begins to change. It may crack and waver. A girl's breasts and hips begin to develop. She gets her period. Teens may not be prepared for these changes. They may not understand exactly what is happening to their body. They may be uncomfortable with their new body for a while.

Hormones, the chemicals that control growth and development, also affect a teen's personality. The same hormones that make a teen grow also can cause mood swings, anger, and sensitivity. This may cause a teen to react more extremely to things. For example, a teen may be very upset by something that an adult thinks is no big deal.

Not everyone goes through puberty at the same time. Teens who go through puberty earlier may feel awkward and be afraid of ridicule. Girls whose breasts develop early may be targets of harassment. Teens who go through puberty later also may feel embarrassed. They may be teased because they are shorter or smaller than others are. They may not be as good at sports. They may feel left out of some activities, such as dating.

Trish Feels Left Out

Trish, Liz, and Zina have been best friends for years. But now, Trish is afraid that her friends are growing apart. Liz and Zina have started getting their period and wearing bras. They go shopping for clothes and makeup together and talk about guys all the time. Trish doesn't have anything to say during these conversations. Sometimes Liz and Zina go on double dates together.

Trish feels like such a baby. Sometimes, she wishes that she had a boyfriend. Other times, she wishes she and her friends could go back to how they were before.

Romance and Sexuality

During puberty, teens become physically able to reproduce, or have children. Their body begins to get ready for sex. The body usually is ready for sex before the mind and emotions are. The body may send confusing or even frightening messages. Teens also begin to be interested in others romantically. However, they may not know how to act around people they are interested in. They may not know how to date. They may feel pressure to date before they are ready. They may be uncomfortable with their sexuality.

Personal Changes

During puberty, a teen's personality also changes. A teen is moving from childhood to adulthood. This is a difficult place to be.

Becoming Self-Conscious

Because of the changes that happen in puberty, most teens are very self-conscious. They often feel like everyone is looking at them. They may exaggerate their own flaws. Teens may be embarrassed even when no one else notices the flaws. Most teens are very sensitive to criticism and may be easily offended.

Problems With Parents

A teen's relationship with his or her parents often changes. Teens often are critical of their parents. They may criticize their parents' values or actions. It is normal to want more independence. However, teens may feel like they are supposed to push their parents away. It is an unhealthy myth that teens don't need their parents as much as they used to. Teens still need their parents' support, but in different ways. Pushing parents away can make a teen feel lost. It may make peer pressure stronger.

Relying on Friends

Friends are very important to most teens. They turn to their friends for support and advice. Criticism from friends can be extremely hurtful. Most teens are afraid of being different and not having friends. This makes pressure from friends to conform very strong.

Scapegoating Others

Some people who feel awkward and unsure may try to make others feel bad. They may make fun of others. This may make them feel better about themselves. They may pressure others to do things. This may make them feel more powerful and in control.

"Peer pressure is all about manipulation—it's not about friendship. People who pressure you into doing stuff don't care about you; they care about their own power trip."
—Joshua, a teen who wrote about peer pressure on-line

Feeling scared and confused is normal. Some people, however, don't like to admit that they are afraid. They don't want to seem different or weak. So they find someone else to pick on or harass. They are really punishing this person for their own fears and worries. This is called scapegoating.

Lincoln Feels Lost

Lincoln and Marcus had been best friends in grade school. But Marcus moved the summer before seventh grade. Lincoln didn't really have any other friends. He felt lost. There were so many kids at school, but it seemed like he didn't fit in anywhere.

Then this guy, Lamar, started talking to Lincoln, and being really nice to him. Lamar was in a local gang, and he told Lincoln how great it was, how the gang was like a big family. He told Lincoln how the other gang members were such close friends. Lincoln knew that the gang was really violent, but he was tired of being lonely. He joined, and at first he loved the feeling of belonging to something.

Social Changes

Middle school is a big change from grade school. Teens come in contact with more people in classes, hallways, clubs, and teams. There is less adult supervision than in grade school. All this can make teens feel overwhelmed and lost. Belonging to a group may make teens feel more secure.

Schools may mix many kinds of people in the classroom. However, teens may separate themselves based on race or culture. For example, African-American students may sit together at lunch. Teens also may separate themselves based on a common activity. For example, people who play the same sport may hang out together. Teens usually find groups of people who are like them. "Jocks," "preps," and "goths" are examples of common types of groups.

Some groups are very exclusive. Cliques only allow certain people to belong. Crowds are less exclusive. You may hang out with people from several different crowds. Most teens, however, want to belong to some kind of group. Sometimes a teen may talk, dress, or behave in certain ways in order to be accepted by others. Some groups put a lot of pressure on their members to conform.

Points to Consider

What do you think is most stressful about puberty?

Why do you think that many teens may have problems with their parents?

How are your friends similar to you? How are they different?

What are the main cliques or crowds at your school? What separates one group from another? How are they alike?

Chapter Overview

Peer relations are important for social, emotional, and psychological growth.

Peer pressure may help teens do well in school, sports, work, or service.

Peer pressure may be used for such positive activities as peer tutoring, peer counseling, and peer mediation.

Chapter 3

Is Peer Pressure All Bad?

When people think of peer pressure, they often think of something negative. People blame peer pressure for problems such as teenage drinking, drug use, smoking, sex, or vandalism, the destruction of others' property. It is true that peer pressure can cause problems. Sometimes conforming to the crowd can get you into trouble. However, peer pressure is a part of growing up. Some peer pressure is positive.

Why You Need Some Peer Pressure

Adolescence is a time when teens learn how to be adults. Part of being adult is knowing how to get along with others. Part of it is knowing yourself. Peers help you learn to be adult. They help you grow socially, emotionally, and psychologically.

Social Skills

Everyone needs social skills to deal with people throughout life. Peer pressure helps everyone learn how to behave around others. It teaches people what kind of behavior is polite and appropriate.

Your friends and peers now give you a chance to learn important social skills. You are learning how to relate to others in a mature and healthy way. Your peers help you learn how to treat people with respect. They help you learn how to get along with others and how to meet new people. They even help you learn how to deal with people who don't like you or who disagree with you.

"No man is an island, entire of itself; every man is a piece of the continent, a part of the main."
—John Donne (1572–1631)

Emotional Growth

Humans are social creatures. They often need others around them in order to be happy. You need someone to talk with on your own level. Your peers are concerned about many of the same things you are. They share many of your feelings.

Peers also help you learn appropriate ways to express your emotions. You learn what to do when others have needs or wants that conflict with yours. Peers and friends help you learn to be sympathetic and understanding. They help you think about how others are feeling.

Psychological Health

People who have good psychological health have a strong sense of identity. They understand their mind and emotions. They know how to deal with problems in healthy ways. They do not do things that hurt themselves or others.

An important part of being a teen is figuring out who you are. This is very difficult. No one can do this alone. You need to be able to try out different things and see how others react. You need other people to talk with and work through issues with. You can look at your peers and decide if what they do is right for you. Part of how we learn about ourselves is through other people. Even negative experiences help us make better choices in the future.

Sadao Joins the Team

Sadao's friends ask him to sign up for the track team with them.
Sadao says no. He says he doesn't really like sports. But his friends insist, and finally he gives in.

Soon, Sadao realizes that he really likes to be in shape. He loves to compete and be part of a team. He decides to try out for the soccer team and ends up being a star player.

Sadao thanks his friends for making him join track. He had never really tried sports. He just assumed that he wouldn't like them. He is glad they pushed him to try something new.

Positive Pressure

Some peer pressure helps teens do their best. Many teens become better athletes because they know their teammates depend on them. Some teens study hard because they want to keep up with their classmates. Other teens may volunteer for service projects because their friends expect it. Friends can be a positive influence on you and help you achieve more.

Pressure from others may encourage teens to try new things. For example, you may not have considered trying out for the school play. However, friends may urge you to try out with them. You may really enjoy acting, but you might not have tried it without a little pressure from others.

"I have eight little brothers and sisters, so I'm used to settling arguments. I was excited to hear that our school was starting a peer mediation program. All of the peer mediators went through training together, and now when students have problems with each other, they can come to one of us. Our job is to listen to both sides of the story. We help them work out a compromise or solution. It's a great feeling to help your friends and classmates. And I know the skills I've learned will help me all my life."
—Kha, age 16

Using Peer Pressure to Help Others

There are programs that use peer pressure for positive activities. Some schools have peer tutoring programs. Both the students who seek help and the tutors benefit from better grades and self-esteem. A peer counseling program teaches teens how to help other teens with their problems. Teens might prefer to get advice from a peer rather than from an adult. Some drug resistance programs let teens educate other teens about the dangers of drug use.

Peer mediation programs train teens to resolve problems among their classmates. The peer mediators learn conflict resolution, or peaceful ways to end fights. Two teens who can't talk with each other may be able to talk with another teen. That third person can help them reach a solution.

Points to Consider

Why do you think peer pressure is seen as negative?

How can friends help you learn about yourself?

Have you ever experienced positive pressure from peers? What happened?

Why do you think teens might like to get advice from other teens?

Chapter Overview

The media encourages teens to think that they need certain products, such as clothes or shoes, to be happy and popular.

Some trends and fads are harmless. Others may be expensive, dangerous, or permanent.

Most teens feel pressure to look attractive. They often have unrealistic expectations for themselves.

Many girls and women feel pressure to be thin. They may have eating disorders.

Chapter 4

The Pressure to Look Right

I go to this school where some of the students have a lot of money. These guys wear really expensive shoes, and it seems like a different brand is in every month. They have lots of clothes, expensive shirts, jeans, and sunglasses. They even wear trendy baseball hats. My mom doesn't make that much money. I'm sure people notice that I wear the same clothes all the time and never have the right label. One time this guy started giving me a hard time because my jeans were this cheap brand. Mom says that jeans are jeans, and it doesn't matter what brand my clothes are. But I think it does.

Dimitri, Age 15

Did You Know?

Uniforms aren't just for private schools anymore. Some public schools now require students to wear uniforms. Parents said their teens faced too much pressure to wear the right kind of clothes.

Having the Right Look

Teens often feel great pressure to dress and look a certain way. Some of that pressure comes from images in the media. Magazines, television programs, and movies show people wearing fashionable clothes. Advertising tries to influence teens to buy things. It tells them that they need certain items or brands to be attractive and cool. Some teens wear clothes with logos so everyone will know that they have the right clothes.

Peer pressure may make these messages stronger. Teens who do not wear the right clothes may feel like they don't fit in. They may fear that others will laugh at them if they wear a cheaper version of a popular brand. People may tease them if they are out of style.

Trends and Fads

Some trends and fads are harmless. For example, cutting or coloring your hair a certain way won't matter much in the long run. However, following every trend in clothing and music may get expensive. You or your parents may not be able to afford new things every time trends change.

Some fads are more serious. For example, tattoos and body piercing change a person's body forever. They are still on your body after styles change. Some people are happy with their tattoos. Others, however, regret marking their body forever.

Pressure to Look Attractive

People often judge others based on looks. It is natural to want to look nice. However, too much emphasis on looks may be unhealthy. It may cause people to feel stressed or lose their self-confidence.

Unrealistic Expectations

People often have unrealistic expectations, or standards, for themselves. Teens often worry about being attractive because they have acne, sweat a lot, smell bad, or wear braces or glasses. Many of these things are natural when teens go through puberty. They are caused by the new hormones in a teen's body. Teens may think they are too short, too tall, too thin, or too heavy.

Deodorants and special face cleansers can help. It is also important to bathe or shower daily, get regular exercise, and eat healthy foods. However, the key to looking attractive is being comfortable with yourself.

"If you're not feeling good about you, then what you're wearing on the outside doesn't mean a thing."
—Leontyne Price

The media may increase the pressure to look attractive. The media helps create unrealistic expectations for people. Most people do not look like actors and models. Professional makeup artists and hairstylists spend hours making an actor look good. However, many people compare themselves with actors and models anyway. As a result, they may feel fat or ugly. They may feel unattractive because their clothes aren't as nice as the ones that actors wear.

Pressure From Peers

There is a lot of peer pressure to be physically attractive. People often assume that physically attractive people are smarter, more talented, and more socially powerful. This is not true. Attractive people may be mean or not very bright. Teens may think they must be attractive in order to be popular. However, most people prefer to be friends with people who are friendly and accepting of others.

Teens often have a narrow idea of what is attractive. Teens who do not fit this ideal may be teased.

There's this girl in my class named Maura. **Kesia, Age 16** The guys make mooing noises at her like she's a cow. When she sits down at lunch, people make pig sounds. I've watched, and she hardly eats anything. Sometimes they make her cry. I've even heard girls making comments about her. She isn't even really that heavy. But it seems like the guys at my school only like the super-skinny girls. The really thin girls get asked out all the time. If you don't look like a model or someone like that, then they say you're fat.

It makes me so mad. I did a report on anorexia, and I found out it can kill you. I wonder if the guys ever think about what they're doing when they tease Maura.

The Pressure to Be Thin

Girls especially are often teased because of how they look. Girls and women may feel enormous pressure to be thin. Some of this pressure comes from peers. The media often shows women who are very thin. The average model weighs 25 percent less than the average woman. Girls may see these images and think they are overweight. They may think they must be thin to be attractive to guys. Some teens may accept the media's standard of an ideal body. They might make fun of girls who don't meet it. Even girls who are at a healthy weight may be called fat. Some girls start dieting in elementary school.

Some girls and women may get an eating disorder. They may have anorexia, which means they starve themselves. Others eat a lot, but then purge to get rid of the food. They may force themselves to throw up, take laxatives, or overexercise. This eating disorder is called bulimia. Most people with anorexia or bulimia are female.

Males may not feel as much pressure as females to be thin. However, they may think they have to have big muscles. They may be pressured to be athletic and strong. They may be teased for being a wimp or a sissy. Some males may become addicted to lifting weights. They may take steroids to help them get big muscles.

Peer Pressure

Points to Consider

Why do you think that many teens wear the same kinds of clothes?

How do you feel when you compare yourself with your friends? with actors or models?

Do you think people assume that attractive individuals are better people? Why? What do you think when you first meet an attractive person?

Why do you think girls feel more pressure to be thin than boys do?

Chapter Overview

Many teens feel strong pressure to fit in and do what everyone else does.

People in groups often do things they would not do alone.

Some pressure helps teens to do their best.

Some pressure encourages negative behavior, such as cruelty to others, dating too early, or other dangerous or illegal activities.

Chapter 5

The Pressure to Act Cool

Keisha, the star basketball player, gets a belly button ring. Soon, several other players get their navel pierced, too. One of them asks Margo why she doesn't get a belly button ring. Margo says that she thinks they're kind of silly and she doesn't want one. Her teammate tells Keisha what Margo said. Keisha is mad that Margo criticized her.

Now Keisha and the other players are harassing Margo. They mock her and say she is scared to get her navel pierced. Sometimes Margo wishes that she had just gotten her navel pierced. She thinks she should have known that criticizing the most popular girl on the team was a mistake.

Many teens feel pressure to be cool. Being cool means different things to different people and different groups. You and your friends may not use the word *cool*. Maybe you say *phat, sharp, hot,* or *tight*. Those words all mean the same thing. They mean acting in the way that you and your friends think is right.

It is normal to want to do the right thing at the right time. No one wants to be laughed at for something they do. Most teens want to fit in with others. You may be harassed if you go against your friends or your crowd.

Keeping Up Your Reputation

Sometimes being in a group makes people act differently. For example, teens in a group may harass another teen. If those teens were alone, however, they would not tease anyone. Sometimes they don't want others to think they are weak. Sometimes they are showing off for their friends.

Teens may want their friends to think of them in a certain way. They may want to have a certain reputation. So they do things in front of others to create or keep that reputation. For example, a teen may want a reputation as someone who doesn't care about school. So he or she complains about school to friends and talks back to teachers. He or she may do all the homework, but keep that a secret. Actions only affect a reputation if others know about them. A reputation needs an audience.

Changing Behavior

Peer pressure helps some teens do their best. Friends may encourage you to do well in school or in sports. You may be encouraged to try new things because of peer pressure. You may feel pressure to get involved in a certain club or service project.

Peer pressure also may push some teens to rebel. It is normal for teens to challenge their parents and other authority figures. In order to figure out who you are, you need to question some rules. This is a healthy part of growing up. Sometimes, however, peer pressure has negative—and permanent—consequences.

Sometimes pressure causes teens to act up in class and get in trouble. Sometimes it encourages teens to be cruel to others. For example, everyone may make fun of a certain student at your school. You may not know the student, but you still may join in when others make fun of the person.

"There's this girl in my class that everyone makes fun of. People are always trying to make her cry. One day I came up behind her and pushed her into this big puddle. She had mud all over her. Lots of people saw and started pointing and laughing. I felt pretty good, until I saw the look on her face. She was trying not to cry, but she was totally ashamed.

"I was so ashamed of myself. I didn't even know her. I just picked on her because everyone else did. She never did anything bad to me. She never did anything bad to anyone. I don't even know why everyone hates her so much."
—Greg, age 15

If you have friends who drop out of school, you may be more likely to drop out, too. Your peers may pressure you to skip classes, cheat on tests, talk back to teachers, or quit school.

I really want to do well in school. I want to be a doctor someday, so I need to earn a **Maria, Age 16** scholarship for college. My mom tries her best to encourage me, but my friends think that homework is a waste of time. They don't care about school at all. They're more interested in guys and partying. They think I'm crazy for working so hard. They tell me to have more fun, that I'm missing out. They always want me to cut classes and shoot up with them. A couple of them have dropped out because they got pregnant.

It seems like they've just given up. But I don't want to give up. I get really discouraged, though. Sometimes I look at them and I wonder why I think I can be any different.

It may seem like everyone is having sex. However, about half of all teens have never had sex by age 18.

Dating and Sex

You may feel like everyone else is dating and having sex. You may feel like you are missing out on something great. You may be pressured into dating before you are ready. A dating partner, your friends, or your peers may pressure you to have sex.

You probably know sex can have serious consequences. You may get pregnant or get someone else pregnant. You may get a sexually transmitted disease like HIV or herpes. You may regret having sex before you are ready. Dating or having sex too early can damage your relationships with your same-sex friends and future dating partners. It's important not to date or have sex before you are ready.

Risky Behavior

Sometimes teens pressure others to take harmful risks. Teens may dare each other to shoplift or commit vandalism. In some extreme cases, teens may pressure each other to injure or assault others. You may be with a group that does something illegal or dangerous. Even if you don't participate, you may feel pressure to go along and not protest.

Teens may join gangs in order to fit in. However, gangs pressure members to do illegal and violent things. Gang members commit more than 11 violent acts per year. Even having delinquent friends can cause pressure. Teens whose peers are often in trouble with the law commit more than five violent acts in a year. By contrast, most teens who have nondelinquent peers do not commit any violent acts.

Teens may feel pressure because they think everyone else is drinking, smoking, or doing drugs. You may be pressured to ride with a driver who has been drinking. You may not have another ride home. The driver may tell you that he or she isn't really drunk. Others may laugh at you for making a big deal out of it.

No Big Deal?

Peer pressure is a big deal whenever it makes someone do something they don't want to do. It is a big deal when it leads to risky behavior. Peer pressure can take some of your control away. You may take a risk that you don't really want to take. You may hurt yourself or someone else. You may have to face the consequences of something you didn't even really want to do. These consequences may last your whole life.

Points to Consider

What are some things you and your friends consider cool?

How do you treat teens whom you do not consider cool?

Have peers ever pressured you to do something you didn't want to? How did you feel?

Do you think you put pressure on others to act a certain way? How do you do that?

Chapter Overview

Peer pressure can cause tremendous stress.

Some ways to say no to pressure include being direct, thinking of a creative excuse, or avoiding uncomfortable situations.

Trying new things and meeting new people may help teens resist peer pressure.

Your parents or another trusted adult may be able to help.

Thinking about the goals you have for yourself and your future may help you overcome peer pressure.

Chapter 6

Dealing With Peer Pressure

Dave dreads going to school now. A group of popular athletes has started picking on him. They call him a sissy and a queer. They push him around in the locker room after gym class. Dave has never been very athletic, but fearing the harassment makes him even clumsier.

Dave Dreads School

Dave doesn't know why these guys harass him. He barely knows them. All he knows is that he is miserable. He can hardly eat. He wakes up every morning tense and sick to his stomach. He wishes he could skip school, but he knows that would just cause more problems.

Peer pressure can be very stressful. Intense pressure may make people physically sick. Some people have trouble sleeping. Others may overeat or lose their appetite. Some get headaches or feel sick to their stomach. Others feel tense or nervous all the time.

Peer pressure may also cause emotional pain. Teens who face a lot of pressure may become depressed and lose their self-confidence. It can be hard to feel good about yourself when others put you down. You may begin to accept your peers' unkind opinion of you. For example, a teen who is teased about her weight may end up thinking of herself as fat. She may not be overweight, but she may feel that she is anyway.

Handling the Stress

You can learn to handle the stress of peer pressure. Try different things until you find something that works for you. You might try deep breathing exercises. Take a deep breath and hold it for a few seconds. Exhale slowly. As you breathe out, think about blowing out the tension that you feel.

Exercise helps many people deal with stress. Exercise can calm you down and improve your mood. Regular exercise may help you get less upset over future stress. Being in shape may improve your confidence. Find some activity that you like doing, such as running, hiking, or swimming. Even a brisk walk can help. You can exercise alone or with a friend.

Listening to music that you like may help. Some people find yoga or meditation relaxing. Other people keep a journal. Putting your feelings on paper can be a big relief.

Try New Things

Sometimes it helps to try new activities and meet new people. You could introduce yourself to new students at school. If you find it difficult to talk to new people, it may help to join a group. For example, you could try band, the school newspaper, the yearbook, an athletic team, or a service organization.

You might want to join a group outside of school. Organizations like the YMCA may offer programs or classes that interest you. You might volunteer at a local child care center, pet shelter, or homeless shelter. Whatever you do, you will probably meet new people with whom you will have something in common. Keeping busy may help you feel less lonely or pressured. Learning a new skill or helping others can help you feel better about yourself.

Toni's New Hobby

Toni feels lonely. So she joins the local chapter of Habitat for Humanity. This national organization builds homes for families who can't afford to buy a house. She meets some great people and discovers that she really likes woodworking.

Toni decides to take a class in carpentry. There she meets Tomas, and they start to date. Toni and Tomas plan to volunteer together on the next Habitat house.

"When you say no to something, don't argue with the other people. That may just make them think that they might be able to change your mind if they keep trying to convince you. You can give your reasons for saying no, but don't get into a big argument about it. Just keep saying no until they get it and stop pushing you."
—Berel, age 17

Saying No

If you are facing direct pressure to do something that you don't want to do, there are many ways to say no. The following strategies may help you resist pressure. Try the ones that you feel comfortable with. Just because you went along with something once doesn't mean you can't say no now.

Be direct.

Talk with the teens who pressure you. Explain that you don't want to do what they want. Be confident, but try not to put them on the defensive.

Being direct can be hard. You may want to practice what to say when you're alone. This may make it easier to say it to others.

Plan ahead.

If you can, avoid uncomfortable or high-pressure situations. If you know that you will be in a difficult situation, plan ahead to make things easier. For example, you may know there will be drinking at a party. You could volunteer to stay sober and be the driver for your friends if you have your license. You can make sure that you have money for a cab or someone to call in case you want to leave.

Find a creative excuse.

You may not feel comfortable saying no directly. It may help to think of a good excuse. It's okay to use your parents as an excuse. For example, you may be out with friends who urge you to break your curfew. You could say that your parents have threatened to ground you if you aren't home on time.

Make a joke.

Sometimes a joke can be a nonthreatening way to ease the pressure.

Bette's friends urge her to skip class **Bette Makes a Joke** with them. She doesn't want to hurt their feelings, but she doesn't want to skip class either. "I can't skip English," she says. "I live for the sight of Mr. Caldwell. He's so hot!" Her friends laugh because they think the teacher is old and boring. No one has a crush on him. But they don't push Bette to skip class. Instead, they make jokes with her about it.

Fake it for now.

Sometimes it is okay to pretend to go along with things that you don't want to do. This gives you time to think of a better way to deal with the pressure. For example, you may not want to drink at a party. You can dump your beer down the toilet and fill the can with water. No one will know you're not drinking alcohol.

This strategy works for some people, but it makes others feel more tense. It works best as a temporary solution.

Talk with your parents.

Sometimes it may seem like your parents don't understand what you're going through. They may seem to downplay the pressure that you face. However, adults know what it's like to be pressured. They were teens once, too. They can tell you what it was like for them and how they dealt with it. They may be able to suggest some ways to cope with pressure. You can talk with a parent, another relative, a school counselor, or another trusted adult.

My friends usually have parties whenever **Janine, Age 16** their parents are out of town. If they call to invite me, I'll wave my dad over near the phone. I'll yell to ask if I can go over to their house, but I'll shake my head no. That way my dad knows to say no so they can hear it. Then my friends don't push me to go.

My dad and I had a big talk about parties and stuff like that. Some of my friends sneak around and lie to their parents. I think it's so much easier to have my dad on my side.

Trust your instincts.

You may have a feeling that something others are pushing you to do is wrong. Trust that feeling. Even if you can't explain it or if others argue with you, listen to your instincts. Don't do anything that doesn't feel right. If others have to convince you to do something, maybe you don't really want to do it.

Teen Talk

"I'm not sure what I want to do after high school. But I do know that I want to go to college. I don't want anything to interfere with my goals. I study hard, and I don't drink or do drugs. I don't even want to have sex. Some of my friends think I'm silly and uptight. And sometimes I wonder if I'm missing out. But this way I'm not closing any doors for myself. A little fun now isn't worth my dreams. And to tell you the truth, I'm not sure that the people who party and have sex are having that much more fun than I am."
—Aisha, age 16

Think about your future.

You may know how to say no. However, you also have to want to say no. Think about your goals. Think about what you want for your future. When you feel pressure to do something, think about how that action might affect your future. If you aren't sure what you want, it may be a good idea to keep your options open. You can choose not to do something that might limit you. Some things that seem like fun now may have permanent consequences.

Sometimes people will tell you just to be yourself. This can be very hard when you are a teen. You may not be sure exactly who you are. Do you want someone else making that decision for you? You can choose to resist pressure to do things you don't want to do. You can avoid doing things that may have negative consequences. That way, you give yourself time to figure out what you want and who you are.

People eventually will respect you for sticking to your goals and standing up for yourself. They may not respect you for giving in to pressure.

Peer Pressure

Points to Consider

What do you do when friends urge you to do something that you don't want to?

How do you handle peer pressure? How could you handle it better?

What are your goals for the future? What career would you like to have? Do you want a family? Where would you like to live? What do you need to do to achieve your goals?

What actions now might make it harder to achieve your goals? Have you ever felt pressure to do any of those things?

Chapter Overview

Everyone feels peer pressure.

Some peer pressure comes from inside.

The friends you choose affect the pressure you feel.

Peer pressure changes as you get older.

You can handle peer pressure.

Chapter 7

Important Stuff to Remember

Friends are an important part of everyone's life. What your friends and peers think of you matters to you. Peer pressure is part of being a teen. However, you can deal with the pressure. Remember:

1. Everyone feels peer pressure.

It is normal to compare yourself with your peers. It is normal to worry about whether others like you. Almost everyone feels pressure to conform in order to be accepted. No matter how popular a teen is, he or she feels some pressure. Even the people who harass and pressure others feel pressured themselves.

2. Some pressure comes from inside.

You may put a lot of pressure on yourself. Teens may be influenced by what they think everyone else is doing. However, they often are wrong about what others think or do. For example, teens usually overestimate how many teens smoke, drink, do drugs, or have sex. A teen may think that most teens smoke. In reality, less than 20 percent of teens smoke.

3. The friends you choose affect the pressure you feel.

Your friends and peers will have some influence on you. This influence can be positive or negative. How they influence you depends on what kind of friends you have. What qualities would you want in an ideal friend? Do your friends now have those qualities? What are your goals for the future? Do your friends have similar goals? Do they respect your goals?

Peer Pressure

Teens often change friends. Most teens don't have the same friends at graduation that they did in seventh grade. If the friends you have pressure you to be something you don't want to be, you can choose new friends. You also can add to the friends you already have. Find people who support you in what you do. Friends are important, but you also have to be a friend to yourself.

4. Peer pressure changes.
Experts say that peer pressure is strongest in middle school. This is when puberty usually starts. Teens are most unsure of themselves at this time. Teens may find a lot of security and comfort in belonging to a group. This can make pressure very strong.

As you move toward graduation, you may notice that cliques loosen up. Teens may begin to be more open to more people. As teens get older they have a better sense of who they are. They may find cliques limiting instead of supporting. They are more confident and better able to resist pressure. Most teens say that pressure is less intense in their later years of high school.

5. You can handle peer pressure.

Peer pressure can be painful, but you can learn to cope. You don't have to go along with the crowd. You can learn to handle stress, become independent, and make your own choices.

The stress and pain that you feel now can help you in the future. The skills you develop now to cope with pressure will be useful later. Dealing with peer pressure may make you think about how you put pressure on others. You may become more sympathetic. You may be a better friend to someone else.

Points to Consider

What does it mean to be a friend to someone else?

What does it mean to be a friend to yourself?

How do you deal with people who don't like you or pressure you? How might you deal with them better?

How do you think peer pressure might change as you get older?

Glossary

adolescence (ad-uh-LESS-unss)—the time between childhood and adulthood, when a person is more grown-up than a child but is not yet an adult

anorexia (an-uh-REK-si-uh)—an eating disorder in which people starve themselves

bulimia (buh-LEE-mee-uh)—an eating disorder in which people overeat and then purge, or throw up, take laxatives, or overexercise to get rid of the food

clique (KLEEK)—a small exclusive group of people who consider themselves friends

conform (kuhn-FORM)—to behave in the same way as everyone else or in the way that others expect

delinquent (di-LING-kwuhnt)—a person who is often in trouble with the law

harass (huh-RASS)—to bother, disturb, or upset another person

hormone (HOR-mohn)—a natural chemical in the body that controls growth and body functions

manipulate (muh-NIP-yuh-late)—to influence people in a clever way so that they do what you want them to do

ostracize (OS-tra-size)—to exclude someone and make that person feel like an outsider

psychological (sye-kuh-LOJ-uh-kul)—relating to the mind, emotions, and human behavior

puberty (PYOO-bur-tee)—the time when a person's body changes from a child's to an adult's

reputation (rep-yuh-TAY-shuhn)—a person's character as seen or judged by others

scapegoat (SKAPE-goht)—someone who is unfairly made to take the blame for something

stress (STRESS)—worry, strain, or pressure

vandalism (VAN-duhl-iz-uhm)—damage or destruction of other people's property

For More Information

Folkers, Gladys, and Jeanne Engelmann. *Taking Charge of My Mind and Body: A Girls' Guide to Outsmarting Alcohol, Drugs, Smoking, and Eating Problems.* Minneapolis: Free Spirit, 1997.

Hipp, Earl, and Pamela Espeland. *Fighting Invisible Tigers: A Stress Management Guide for Teens.* Minneapolis: Free Spirit, 1995.

Kaplan, Leslie. *Coping With Peer Pressure.* New York: Rosen, 1996.

McCoy, Kathy, and Charles Wibbelsmann. *Life Happens: A Teenager's Guide to Friends, Failure, Sexuality, Love, Rejection, Addiction, Peer Pressure, Families, Loss, Depression, Change, and Other Challenges of Living.* New York: Berkeley, 1996.

Scott, Sharon. *How to Say No and Keep Your Friends.* Amherst, MA: Human Resource Development Press, 1997.

Useful Addresses and Internet Sites

Anorexia Nervosa and Related Eating
Disorders, Inc. (ANRED)
PO Box 5102
Eugene, OR 97405
www.anred.com

Partnership for a Drug-Free America
405 Lexington Avenue, 16th floor
New York, NY 10174
www.drugfreeamerica.org

Planned Parenthood Federation of America
810 Seventh Avenue
New York, NY 10019
1-800-230-7526
www.teenwire.com

Planned Parenthood Federation of Canada
1 Nicholas Street, Suite 430
Ottawa, ON K1N 7B7
CANADA

Students Against Drunk Driving (SADD)
PO Box 800
Marlboro, MA 01752
www.saddonline.com

Center for Disease Control Tobacco
Information and Prevention Source
www.cdc.gov/tobacco
Information about tobacco use, with a special
page for teens

Kids Help Phone Line
1-800-668-6868
Hotline staffed by counselors 24 hours a day to
help Canadian youth

Teen Line
1-800-743-1672
Hotline staffed by teens to deal with such
problems as suicide, drugs, pregnancy, and
eating disorders

Index

acne, 14, 31
activities, trying new, 39, 47
alcohol, 21, 42, 49, 50, 51, 56
anorexia, 33, 34
appearance, 31, 32. *See also* clothes

behaviors, changing, 39
belong, needing to, 18–19, 57
body hair, 14
body piercing, 31, 37
breast development, 14, 15
bulimia, 34

cheating, 6, 40
clothes, 6, 7, 14, 15, 29, 30, 32
conforming, 5, 17, 19, 55
consequences, 40, 42, 52
cool, pressure to be, 30, 38
coping, 58
criticism, 16, 17, 37
curfew, 49

dares, 10
dating, 7, 15, 16, 41
depression, 46
double-dating, 15
drugs, 6, 21, 26, 40, 42, 56

eating disorders, 34. *See also* anorexia;
    bulimia
emotional growth, 23
emotional pain, 46
exercise, 46

fads, 30–31
feeling
    different, 10, 13
    embarrassed, 8, 9, 14, 15, 16
    guilty, 9
    lonely, 47
    scared and confused, 18
    self-conscious, 11, 13, 16
    stupid, 9
    unsure, 13
    upset, 14
fitting in, 7, 11, 18, 30, 38
friends, 6, 8, 9, 10, 15, 23, 38, 40, 55
    choosing, 56–57
    relying on, 17
future, 52, 56, 58

gangs, 18, 19, 42
goals, 52, 56
guilt games, 9

harassment, 8, 10, 15, 32, 37, 38, 45,
    55
hormones, 14, 31

instincts, 51

journal, 47

making fun of people, 6, 8, 10, 14, 17,
    39, 40. *See also* name-calling
media, 30, 32, 34
mediation, 47

Index continued

money, 29
music, 30, 47

name-calling, 8, 34, 45
no, saying, 48–52

ostracization, 9

parents, 17, 30, 39, 49, 50
parties, 40, 49, 50, 51
peer counseling program, 26
peer mediation programs, 26
peer pressure,
    definition of, 5–6
    kinds of, 6–7
    positive, 22–26
    recognizing, 10–11
    ways teens feel, 8–10
peers, 6, 22–23, 32, 34, 55. *See also*
    friends
peer tutoring programs, 26
period, 14, 15
personality, 13, 14, 16, 32
popular people, 10, 32, 37, 45
pregnancy, 40, 41
property, destruction of, 21
psychological health, 23–24
puberty, 13, 14–15, 17, 31, 57
put-downs, 9

rebel, 39
reputation, 38
romance, 16
rumors, 10

scapegoating, 17–18
school, 14, 18, 19, 30, 39, 57
    dropping out of, 40
    skipping classes, 40, 50
self-confidence, 31, 46, 48
sexual intercourse, 16, 21, 41, 56
sexuality, 16
sexually transmitted diseases (STDs),
    41
shoplifting, 7, 41
smoking, 6, 21, 42, 56
social skills, 22
sports, 15, 24, 39
steroids, 34
stress, 10, 31, 46
    handling, 46–47
studying, 25
sweat, 14, 31

tattoos, 31
trends, 30

vandalism, 21, 41
voice changes, 14
volunteering, 25, 47

weight, 31, 33, 34, 46

yoga, 47